Did Jesus ever see a penguin?

and other questions

Tim Mayfield

Illustrated by Chris Saunderson

Scripture Union

First published 1999
Reprinted 1999, 2002

Scripture Union, 207–209 Queensway, Bletchley, Milton Keynes, MK2 2EB, England.

Email: info@scriptureunionorg.uk
Website: www.scriptureunion.org.uk

ISBN 1 85999 276 5

British Library Cataloguing-in-Publication Data.
A catalogue record of this book is available from the British Library.

Printed and bound in Great Britain by
Creative Print and Design (Wales) Ebbw Vale.

Scripture Union is an international Christian charity working with churches in more than 130 countries, providing resources to bring the good news about Jesus Christ to children, young people and families and to encourage them to develop spiritually through the Bible and prayer.

As well as our network of volunteers, staff and associates who run holidays, church-based events and school Christian groups, we produce a wide range of publications and support those who use our resources through training programmes.

CONTENTS

Who is Jesus?

Imagine the scene. Joseph has taken Mary to Bethlehem. There's no room for them in the inn. So when Mary has a baby boy his cot is a manger – an animal's feeding trough.

Who's the baby?

It's Jesus, of course. Most people know him as a baby in a manger. Not so many people know that when the baby grew up, the things he did and said changed the world.

"He helped me to see again," said Bartimaeus. For years blind Bartimaeus had sat by the roadside. When he met Jesus, all that changed.

"He changed my life," said Zacchaeus. For years Zacchaeus had been a crooked tax collector, stealing people's money. When he met Jesus, he too was changed. He gave away half of what he had.

We read about Jesus in a book of special writings called the Bible. The Bible shows that Jesus was a real person who really lived. It tells us that Jesus did all kinds of special things. So special that ever since, people have asked, "Who is Jesus?"

NOW LOOK AT:

How do we know Jesus isn't just a story?	p16
Who were Jesus' parents?	p17
Did Jesus have brothers and sisters?	p20

What's so special about Jesus?

There was something very special about Jesus. When Jesus came to a town everybody knew about it. Lots of people went to hear what he had to say about God.

Jesus was a natural leader. He knew what he was talking about. Crowds of people came from miles around. They listened to him for days because he acted and spoke with authority.

Jesus had special power, which he used for good. Once he went sailing with his friends. A storm blew up. Jesus' friends were afraid they were going to drown. But when Jesus said to the waves, "Be still," the storm stopped. And his friends said, "Who is this?"

Jesus accepted people. He didn't turn anyone away. It didn't matter what they had done. He loved them for who they were. Once, when Jesus was having dinner, a woman came in. She had done many wrong things. Most of the people there didn't like her. They disapproved of her. She kissed Jesus' feet because he didn't hate her like the others. Jesus told her she would be forgiven for the wrong things she had done.

NOW LOOK AT:

Who is Jesus? p7

Why did Jesus come into our world? p40

Who baptised Jesus? p22

Did Jesus do anything wrong? p75

Where was Jesus born?

It's about two thousand years ago. Imagine you're flying above the earth. You know the baby Jesus has been born, but you don't know where.

You fly down through the clouds and the earth is laid out below you. You're heading towards the Roman Empire – a huge area surrounding the Mediterranean Sea.

"I bet he's been born in Rome," you think. After all, it's the most important place in the empire.

But you're surprised to find yourself flying towards Judea (part of modern-day Israel), a tiny little province on the edge of the empire.

The surprise continues: Jesus isn't even in Jerusalem, the capital of Judea. Instead, you're heading towards Bethlehem, a sleepy little town in the hills.

Bethlehem's packed out. The Romans have decided that every family should go to their birthplace and be counted. You look in all the houses, but there's no sign of Jesus.

Then you're amazed. He's lying in an animals' feeding trough – a manger. Jesus was born in a place where animals were kept, in a sleepy town ruled by foreigners, on the edge of the Roman Empire.

NOW LOOK AT:

What language did Jesus speak?	*p26*
What was the weather like where Jesus lived?	*p27*
Does Jesus still live on earth?	*p87*

Who were the first people to visit baby Jesus?

Imagine something very important has just happened to you. Your favourite team's won the cup. You've won a national competition.

Who are the first people you tell? The people most important to you, of course: your best friends, perhaps your mum or dad.

The birth of Jesus was the most important thing that ever happened. So who were the first people God told about it? Kings and queens? No. Religious people? No way. The first people God told were poor shepherds out in the fields looking after their sheep in the middle of the night.

That says a lot about God. In those days people didn't think much of shepherds. They were poor and uneducated, they did not know much about God and they were not important people.

But God told them first! He sent angels to tell them that there would be "Peace on earth". The shepherds raced down the hills into Bethlehem: simple people, overjoyed to meet Jesus.

NOW LOOK AT:

Who were the Wise Men?	p11
Did Jesus get any birthday presents?	p12
Was being a shepherd a good job?	p41
Is Jesus God's Son?	p15

see Matthew chapter 2, verses 1–12

Who were the Wise Men?

Soon after Jesus was born, "Wise Men" came to visit him. They came from a country to the east of Bethlehem. They came to worship a new baby king. They are sometimes, wrongly, called the Three Kings.

Who were they? The Bible calls them "Magi" (*May-ji*). "Magi" means either "wise men", "priests" or "astrologers" – people who study the stars.

How did they know a new king had been born? They saw a new star. To them, this meant that something special had happened. The "new star" may have been three planets shining together. Around this time Jupiter, Venus and Saturn shone from the same point in the sky. Together, they would have shone very brightly.

The Magi went first to Jerusalem. There they asked King Herod about the new king. Herod was a friend of Julius Caesar. He had been king since 37BC. He was a cruel man and later tried to kill Jesus.

The Magi found out that God's special king would be born in Bethlehem. The star led them there, and they found the baby Jesus.

NOW LOOK AT:

Where was Jesus born? p9
How do we know that Jesus isn't just a story? p16
Who were the first people to visit baby Jesus? p10
Did Jesus have brothers and sisters? p20

Did Jesus get any birthday presents?

We don't know much about birthdays in the time of Jesus. But we do know that soon after he was born he received three special presents.

The presents were brought by the Magi, or Wise Men. The Wise Men brought gold, frankincense and myrrh. Gold is the most precious metal. Frankincense and myrrh are both a kind of gum or resin that oozes from trees, and have a strong, nice smell. In those days, both were expensive perfumes, not the sort of gift for an "ordinary" baby. The gold, frankincense and myrrh may all have been ways of saying "this is God's special king".

There were also other uses for frankincense and myrrh. Frankincense was burned as part of worshipping God in the Temple. Myrrh was used as a medicine and a pain-killer. It was also used as a sweet-smelling spice which was put on dead bodies before they were buried. These presents could have showed that Jesus was God's special priest, and foretold his death.

Whatever the three gifts meant, they were all expensive: worthy things to offer to Jesus.

NOW LOOK AT:

What happened when someone died? p44

Who were the Wise Men? p11

What does the name 'Jesus' mean?

"Jesus" is a name with a meaning. When God's angel told Jesus' mother, Mary, that she was going to have a special baby, he told her to call him Jesus, because he would "save his people from their sins".

"Jesus" means "God to the rescue!" We all do wrong things, and mess up the world God made. Jesus is "God to the rescue!" He forgives us and shows us how to live.

He is also called "Jesus Christ". The name "Christ" is special as well. To understand it, we need to know that in the Bible, when there was a new king, he was "anointed". This meant that in the "king-making" ceremony, special oil was poured over his head. The name "Christ" means "the anointed one".

In a different language the same word is "Messiah". For hundreds of years, God's people had been expecting the Messiah – God's special king. The followers of Jesus Christ say that he is that king, the Messiah.

NOW LOOK AT:

What language did Jesus speak?	*p26*
Who were Jesus' parents?	*p17*
Why did Jesus have to die?	*p85*
Why did Jesus ride a donkey?	*p78*

Was Jesus a real person?

What year is it? Write it in the space below.

What do you think happened __________ years ago that was so special that we take our date from it?

What happened was that Jesus was born – a real man, living at a real time in history.

That's why when his friend Matthew writes about Jesus in the Bible (in Matthew's Gospel in the New Testament), he keeps mentioning the names of real people. Matthew says that Jesus was born when Herod was king. Herod was a real person. The Romans called him "King of the Jews". Archaeologists have dug up coins that say "King Herod".

Matthew says that Jesus died when Pontius Pilate was governor of Judea. Pilate was also a real person. Ancient writings tell us that he became governor in AD26. They tell us that he was a cruel man, who massacred many Jews. In 1961 a stone slab was discovered proving that Pilate had lived in Judea.

So was Jesus a real person? Yes. He lived in a place we can find on the map, at a real time, among real people.

NOW LOOK AT:

How do we know Jesus isn't just a story? p16

Why did Jesus come into our world? p40

Where was Jesus born? p9

Is Jesus God's Son?

Part of the Bible was written hundreds of years before Jesus came. We call that part the Old Testament. The Old Testament tells of the birth of a child who will be called "Mighty God".

That child was Jesus. Hundreds of years after the Old Testament was written, an angel sent from God told Mary, Jesus' mother, that her baby would be called "the Son of God".

The things that Jesus did when he grew up show why. Wherever he went crowds followed him, because he told them about his Father God and about a new way of life. Jesus took certain people away from the crowds. There, in quiet places, he made them better. He healed people with skin diseases. He helped deaf people to hear and blind people to see.

People who were jealous of Jesus killed him. They nailed him to a wooden cross. But three days later God brought him back to life. He wasn't just a man. He was God's Son: the one who came to show us what God is really like.

NOW LOOK AT:

Who were Jesus' parents? p17
Why did Jesus make sick people well? p71
When did Jesus pray? p59
How did Jesus know that God was his Father? p24
Did Jesus ever get tired? p76

How do we know that Jesus isn't just a story?

How do we know that man landing on the moon isn't just a story? Simple. Look in the history books: the first person landed on the moon in 1969.

How do we know that Jesus isn't just a story? We can look into history books, written by people who weren't followers of Jesus.

One of the historians was called Josephus. He wasn't a follower of Jesus. But he tells us that Jesus lived. He tells us about James "the brother of Jesus, the so-called Christ".

Another was Tacitus. He wasn't a follower of Jesus either. But he tells us something about Jesus' death. "Christ... suffered death... at the hands of Pontius Pilate," he wrote.

If Jesus had been just a story, you wouldn't find him in the history books.

If Jesus had been just a story, his followers wouldn't have been executed for insisting he was alive.

Perhaps most important of all, if Jesus had been just a story, then countless men and women down the ages wouldn't have followed him. But they did. And his teaching changed the world.

NOW LOOK AT:

Was Jesus a real person? p14

Is Jesus God's Son? p15

Who were Jesus' parents?

Jesus' mother was called Mary. She lived in a town called Nazareth. She may only have been a teenager when she became Jesus' mother.

Mary was "betrothed" to a man called Joseph, a carpenter. This means that everyone knew they were going to get married. But they lived apart until their wedding day.

During this time, God sent an angel to Mary. The angel explained that she was going to have a special baby. This baby, called Jesus, would be the Son of God and of Mary, so he would be both God and a human being. He would be a great king and would "save" his people. Mary was thrilled. "Though I am poor and ordinary," she said, "one day the whole world will call me blessed."

When Joseph knew that Mary was going to have a baby, he was upset and thought he had better not marry her. But God sent an angel to Joseph to tell him that the baby was God's Son. So Joseph decided to marry Mary after all.

These were the two people who looked after Jesus. They were brave people. They said "yes" to what God wanted them to do.

NOW LOOK AT:

Who were the first people to visit baby Jesus?	*p10*
Who were Jesus' friends?	*p25*
Did Jesus go to school?	*p21*
Who were Jesus' enemies?	*p72*
How did Jesus know that God was his Father?	*p24*

Where did Jesus grow up?

Jesus grew up in the north of the country we now call Israel. The area was called Galilee and he lived in the small town of Nazareth.

In some ways, Galilee was a good place to live. Lots of people lived there and the streams flowing down from the mountains made farming easy. The area was famous for fruit and the Sea of Galilee for fish.

But in other ways, Galilee wasn't so good. Enemy Roman soldiers often marched through on the good roads they had built. And people in the south who lived near Jerusalem mocked the people of Galilee. When one person heard that Jesus was from Nazareth he said, "Nazareth?! Can anything good come from Nazareth?!"

Sadly, the people of Nazareth were the first to reject Jesus. Perhaps because he had grown up there, they could not believe that he was the Son of God. When he claimed to be God's special messenger, they threw him out of the town.

NOW LOOK AT:

Where was Jesus born?	*p9*
What was the weather like where Jesus lived?	*p27*
What was Jesus' house like?	*p23*
What did Jesus eat?	*p29*

Did Jesus go to church?

It might amaze you to know that Jesus never ever went to church! But that's because they didn't have churches in the time of Jesus.

Instead, Jesus went to a building called a synagogue. This is where Jews met on their holy day (Saturday) – the Sabbath – to worship God, read the Scriptures (holy writings) and pray. Today, Jews still meet in synagogues.

In the time of Jesus a synagogue had a wooden platform in the middle of the floor. On the platform there was a reading stand. Behind the reading stand there was a chair.

The holy books (the part of the Bible we now call the Old Testament) were kept in wooden or stone boxes. The books were scrolls, which could be rolled and unrolled. The scroll was put on the reading stand. The reader would stand to read, then sit on the chair to explain what the reading meant.

One day Jesus visited the synagogue at his home town of Nazareth. He stood up and read from the scroll. He sat down to explain it. But the people didn't like what he said and made him leave the town.

NOW LOOK AT:

Who baptised Jesus? p22

Where did Jesus grow up? p18

When did Jesus pray? p59

Did Jesus own a Bible? p42

Did Jesus have brothers and sisters?

Yes. The Bible names his brothers as James, Joseph, Simon and Judas. It also mentions "his sisters". Jesus is described as Mary's "first-born", so all these brothers and sisters were born after Jesus.

Brothers and sisters don't always get on too well. They grow up together and have to share lots of things. Sometimes that leads to trouble.

If you've ever had trouble with brothers and sisters, Jesus knows how you feel. It says in the Bible that "even his own brothers did not believe in him". Later, though, his brother James became a leader in the church.

On another occasion, Jesus was teaching people in a crowded house when his mother and brothers arrived. They tried to take him home, because people were saying Jesus was mad.

When Jesus was told his brothers were outside he asked, "Who are my brothers?" He then answered the question himself: he said that anyone who does what God wants is Jesus' brother or sister.

Think of that! If you do what God wants you to do today... then Jesus is your elder brother!

NOW LOOK AT:

Who were Jesus' friends? p25

What did Jesus wear? p32

Who were Jesus' parents p17

Where did Jesus grow up? p18

Did Jesus go to school?

Yes. We can be almost certain that Jesus went to school. In Jesus' country all boys from about the age of six went to school. In fact, it was against the law to live in a place where there was no school!

If there was no school building in your town, the lessons took place in the open air. There would be no seats. The teacher would stand, with the pupils sitting on the ground in a semi-circle.

First, boys learned to read and write. When they could do that, they moved on to lessons from the Scriptures – the holy books of the Jewish religion, which we now call the Old Testament. From the age of ten to fifteen, students would learn all about religious rules.

So it was nearly all RE! No maths. No science. No sport. No computer studies or technology. And no girls! Girls learned at home from their mothers. You can decide for yourself whether you're happier at your school, or whether you'd like to travel back in time, and go to school with Jesus.

NOW LOOK AT:

What sort of stories did Jesus tell?	*p63*
Did Jesus own a Bible?	*p42*
Why did Jesus use stories to tell people about God?	*p68*
Did Jesus draw cartoons?	*p70*

Who baptised Jesus?

John the Baptist baptised Jesus. John was Jesus' cousin. Like Jesus, he had been born with a special job to do. He was an amazing, powerful man. He lived in the desert. He wore rough clothes made of camel's hair.

Hundreds of people went out into the desert to listen to John. When they heard him talk about God's special Messiah who was coming, many of them realised they had done wrong things and wanted to say sorry to God.

John told them to be baptised in the River Jordan. When they "washed" in the water, it was a way of showing God that the person was sorry for the wrong things they had done, and they wanted to live a new "clean" life. When John told the people that he was preparing the way for the Messiah, he was talking about Jesus.

John was a very brave man. He even told King Herod that what he was doing was wrong. The king didn't like that. He threw John into prison, and later had him beheaded.

NOW LOOK AT:

What happened when Jesus was baptised? p28
What did the name 'Jesus' mean? p13
Did Jesus go to church? p19
What did Jesus say about human beings? p66

What was Jesus' house like?

Most ordinary houses had only one room, split into two levels. In the upper level, on a sort of platform, the family slept. Downstairs, the animals were kept. At night the house would be lit with oil lamps made of clay and filled with olive oil.

The floor would have been made of hard earth. The walls would have been made of earth bricks. The bricks would have been dried in the sun and coated with clay.

Outside, steps led onto the roof, which was flat. The roof was made of wooden beams. On the beams the builders would put branches, then reeds. The whole roof would be covered with clay, then rolled flat.

One day Jesus was teaching the people inside someone's house. There were crowds and crowds of people. Four friends brought a paralysed man to be healed by Jesus. When they couldn't get him into the house, they simply dug down through the roof and let him down on a stretcher. Jesus made him able to walk.

NOW LOOK AT:

Did Jesus have an ordinary job? p45

What did Jesus eat? p29

Why did the wise man build his house upon the rock? p62

Does Jesus still live on earth? p87

How did Jesus know that God was his Father?

When Jesus prayed to God, he called him by a special name – "Abba". In his language "Abba" means "Dad" – and that shows us that Jesus knew and loved God as his Father in a really special way. Some religious people were upset – nobody had called God that before.

In Luke's Gospel we read of something that happened when Jesus was only twelve years old. He had visited Jerusalem for a special festival with his parents and crowds of other people.

On the way home his parents realised he was missing and went back to the temple, where they found him talking with the Jewish teachers. When they told him how worried they had been, all he said was, "Didn't you know I had to be in my Father's house?"

Later when Jesus was baptised, Jesus heard God's voice: "You are my Son. I am pleased with you."

It is clear that Jesus knew from quite an early age that God was his Father. He knew how deeply God loved him. And he told his followers to start their prayers "Abba" – "Our Father".

NOW LOOK AT:

Who is Jesus?	p7
What happened when Jesus was baptised?	p28
What did Jesus tell people about God?	p38
What is the Lord's prayer?	p57

Who were Jesus' friends?

Jesus had three close friends: Peter, James and John; and nine other special friends. They are often known as the twelve disciples. A "disciple" is someone who listens carefully to what a teacher says. Jesus' disciples went with him on his travels, listening to what he said, and helping him in his work.

Peter was a fisherman who left his work to become a follower of Jesus. The night before Jesus died, Peter said he would never let Jesus down. But when Jesus was arrested, Peter was afraid: he lied and said he did not know Jesus. Later, he was sorry. Jesus forgave him, and gave him a new job of leading his followers after he died. Peter never let Jesus down again.

James and John were brothers. They were also fishermen. Jesus gave them a nickname – the "Sons of Thunder". Jesus asked John to look after his mother, Mary, after his death.

The other disciples were Peter's brother Andrew, Philip, Nathanael (sometimes called Bartholomew), Matthew, Simon the Zealot, Thomas, James the son of Alphaeus, Judas son of James and Judas Iscariot, who betrayed him.

Jesus also had many, many other friends mentioned in the Gospels, including Martha, Mary and Lazarus, Mary Magdalene and Nicodemus.

NOW LOOK AT:

Why did people hate tax collectors? p31
Was Jesus ever sad? p69
What was it like being a fisherman? p48
How did Jesus die? p84

see John chapter 19, verses 18–22 and Matthew chapter 27, verses 45,46

What language did Jesus speak?

When Jesus was nailed to a cross, the soldiers nailed a sign above his head. It said, "Jesus of Nazareth, the King of the Jews." The sign was written in three different languages, so that everyone could understand it.

It was written in **Latin** – the language the Roman soldiers spoke.

It was written in **Greek** – the language the New Testament is written in.

The sign was also written in a language called **Aramaic** (*A-ra-may-ic*), the language Jesus spoke. Even though the New Testament is mostly written in Greek, there are several times when the words of Jesus are in Aramaic.

When he's praying at the bedside of a dead girl, Jesus says, "*Talitha koum*" – that's Aramaic for "Little girl, get up."

When he's praying for a deaf and dumb man, Jesus says, "*Ephphatha*" – that's Aramaic for "Be opened."

When he's praying for strength before his arrest, Jesus calls God "*Abba*" – that's Aramaic for "Dad".

And when he was dying on the cross Jesus cried out in Aramaic: "*Eloi, eloi, lama sabachthani*" – "My God, why did you abandon me?"

NOW LOOK AT:

Did Jesus go to school? p21
Where did Jesus grow up? p18
Did Jesus have an ordinary job? p45
How did Jesus die? p84

see Mark chapter 4, verses 37–41

What was the weather like where Jesus lived?

Jesus lived in the country which we now call Israel. Like many Mediterranean countries near Africa, it gets very hot during the day and quite cold at night.

Some of Jesus' stories mention the weather – he told a story about a farmer sowing seeds. Some of the seeds grew and then got scorched by the hot sun. He told a story about people growing grapes. They complained that it was very hot work.

We know it got cold at night because we read that on the night Jesus was arrested, everyone in the temple courtyard was standing around a fire. In the firelight, someone recognised Peter as one of Jesus' friends.

In some parts of the country, big storms would blow up. Jesus and his friends were once on Lake Galilee in a boat. A storm started, and some of them were afraid they would drown.

During some of the storms it would rain very hard. Sometimes whole villages would collapse, because the houses were made of earth bricks.

NOW LOOK AT:

What jobs did people do?	*p37*
Did Jesus ever see a penguin?	*p36*
Why did the wise man build his house upon the rock?	*p62*
What did Jesus wear?	*p32*

What happened when Jesus was baptised?

When Jesus first asked John to baptise him, John refused. John realised that Jesus, unlike every other human being, had never done anything wrong. Jesus was the special person, the Messiah, that all God's people had been waiting for.

John had already baptised hundreds of people who wanted to be forgiven and start afresh – he knew that Jesus did not need to be baptised. But Jesus wanted to identify with the people. So John baptised Jesus, letting him fall back under the water of the River Jordan and lifting him out again.

Then Jesus got out of the water and prayed. As he prayed, something special happened. He saw heaven opening and he saw the Holy Spirit coming to him, in the form of a dove. He heard God's own voice saying, "You are my dear Son. I am very pleased with you."

John the Baptist was very excited. He told people that Jesus was the special person they were waiting for: the Son of God.

NOW LOOK AT:

What's so special about Jesus?	*p8*
Did Jesus do anything wrong?	*p75*
Is Jesus God's son?	*p15*

What did Jesus eat?

Like people the world over, Jesus ate a lot of bread. Villagers would grow their own corn and grind their own flour. In every house, the women baked bread each day.

Jesus and his friends lived near Lake Galilee so there was always fish to eat. They had no fridges then so any fish not eaten was dried and then preserved by rubbing salt into it. It may have been dried salty fish that Jesus used when he fed five thousand people with a boy's packed lunch.

There was plenty of fruit – grapes, figs, dates, pomegranates – and fresh vegetables, lentils and pulses. Olives and olive oil were part of everyday meals, and cheese from goat's and sheep's milk. Meat was only eaten occasionally. The people ate lamb or goat – pork was forbidden by Jewish food laws.

People had to fetch their water from wells, and sometimes it was not very clean. Wine would be the usual drink, made from the grapes which grew everywhere. There was no tea or coffee – and no Coca-Cola!

NOW LOOK AT:

Did people grow their own food?	*p39*
What jobs did people do?	*p37*
What did Jesus wear?	*p32*
What were weddings like in Jesus' day?	*p34*

What did Jesus teach about prayer?

Praying is a two-way "conversation" between you and God. You don't have to talk out loud – you can talk "inside" yourself. One thing's for certain – God doesn't need special long words or old-fashioned language. God knows you and understands you. Talk to God in your own words, in your own way, whenever it suits you.

For Jesus, the most important thing to remember when praying, is that God loves us! God wants to hear our prayers. He's like the best Dad ever. He's like a good shepherd, lovingly looking after his sheep.

Sometimes people think their problems are too tiny for God to notice. Jesus said we were not to worry about that. He said God even knows how many hairs there are on our heads!

Because God loves us, he already knows what we need before we ask him. But he wants us to ask him. Jesus said we should ask God for what we need... and he reminded us not to forget to say "thank you".

NOW LOOK AT:

What did Jesus tell people about God? p38
What is the Lord's prayer? p57
When did Jesus pray? p59
What is a Good Samaritan? p61

Why did people hate tax collectors?

Jesus' enemies were always trying to catch Jesus doing something wrong. One of the things they complained about was that Jesus spent time with tax collectors. But...what's so wrong about tax collectors?

The worst thing about tax collectors was that they collected money for the Romans. The Romans had come hundreds of miles from Rome to conquer the Jews. Now they ruled them by force.

So any Jew who helped the Romans was hated. Tax collectors were even raising money for the Romans! No wonder people hated them. But it got worse. The Romans allowed tax collectors to keep some of the money for themselves. So not only were these people helping the hated Romans, they were even getting rich in the process.

None of that mattered to Jesus. To Jesus, tax collectors were simply people. He chose one of them, Levi, also called Matthew, to be his disciple. He chose to eat with another, Zacchaeus. And Jesus' enemies saw it, couldn't understand that he accepted everyone, and complained about it bitterly.

NOW LOOK AT:

Who were Jesus' friends?	*p25*
Who made Jesus angry?	*p73*
Did Jesus pay taxes?	*p54*
What sort of money did Jesus use?	*p60*

What did Jesus wear?

Jesus probably wore the everyday clothing worn by ordinary men.

First, there was a loincloth or short "skirt" – the very basic clothing worn by a man working outdoors in the hot sun. Over this would be a long cotton shirt (tunic). Jesus spoke about this when he told people to love their enemies. He said if someone took your cloak, you should give him your tunic as well! The tunic usually had a leather belt.

A light cotton headdress protected the face and neck from the hot sun. This was about a metre square and could be folded in different ways. Many people went barefoot but wore leather sandals for longer journeys, which all had to be made on foot, or sometimes by donkey.

In cold weather a cloak woven from either goat's or camel's hair was needed. It was also used as a blanket at night, particularly by people like shepherds who had to sleep out of doors.

NOW LOOK AT:

Was being a shepherd a good job? p41
What was the weather like where Jesus lived? p27
What were weddings like in Jesus' day? p34
How did Jesus travel? p35

Why did Jesus get angry in the temple?

A few days before he was arrested, Jesus visited the great temple in Jerusalem. This was the most important place in the Jewish religion, the place where people could come to worship God. There was a courtyard in the temple where non-Jews were allowed to go and pray. Only they couldn't, because the courtyard had been turned into a noisy market.

Traders were selling cattle, sheep and doves for sacrifices and making lots of money. Others were making a profit by changing people's money into the right coins for the temple tax. This made Jesus very angry because these people were ignoring God.

Jesus made a whip and drove the animals out of the temple. He pushed over the market stalls and scattered the traders' coins. He told them that the temple was a place to meet God, not a place to make money.

This was the last straw for Jesus' enemies. They began looking for a way to kill him.

NOW LOOK AT:

Who made Jesus angry? p73
What did Jesus teach about prayer p30
What sort of money did Jesus use? p60
What happened in the week before Jesus died? p79

What were weddings like in Jesus' day?

Jewish people enjoyed a good wedding – there was feasting and lots of dancing and fun. A village wedding was important – it was a way of celebrating God's goodness and of joining two families together.

Couples were often quite young when they got married; sometimes they were only twelve or thirteen. And they didn't choose each other: that was arranged by their parents, who also had to agree on how much money or property the "wife" would bring with her.

When the wedding day came the bride and groom would put on their very best clothes. Then there'd be a special procession. The man went to the woman's house with a group of friends. They carried her back to the man's house on a special chair called a litter. Everyone else walked alongside the bride, singing, shouting and dancing. This was often at night, so the guests carried little lamps on poles.

When the procession got to the man's house there'd be a great feast. Sometimes the party lasted two weeks, so it's no surprise that when Jesus went to a wedding they ran out of wine.

NOW LOOK AT:

What happened when someone died?	p44
Why did Jesus think that children were important?	p67
Did Jesus go to church?	p19
What did Jesus eat?	p29

How did Jesus travel?

In the time of Jesus there were no cars. But people still had to get about. If you were rich, you might have slaves who would carry you in a litter (a kind of chair on poles). If you were richer still, you might have a carriage, pulled by horses.

But most people weren't rich. So most people walked. Many of the roads were rough and dusty, but some of them were very good. The Romans built good roads to help their soldiers control their empire.

Jesus mostly travelled on foot. It was hot, dusty and tiring. When you arrived at your destination, a servant would come and wash your feet.

It was about seventy miles from Jesus' home town of Nazareth to Jerusalem, the capital city. People walked their journeys in stages of about sixteen Roman miles a day. That's why there were inns along the road, so that people could rest the night before continuing the next day.

P.S. Perhaps you could get out a map and see which town is seventy miles from where you live. Do you think you could walk that far?

NOW LOOK AT:

What was the weather like where Jesus lived? p27

What is a Good Samaritan? p61

Did Jesus ever get tired? p76

Why did Jesus ride a donkey? p78

Did Jesus ever see a penguin?

Jesus lived in a hot country. There were no zoos. And people weren't able to travel the world like they do today. So Jesus probably never actually saw a penguin in Israel.

Among the animals he did see were camels, sheep, goats and chickens. He said that a rich man trying to get to heaven was like a camel trying to squeeze through the eye of a needle. He told a story about God separating good people from bad like a shepherd separating sheep and goats.

At the beginning of the week before he died, he rode into Jerusalem on a donkey. Later that same week, after he had been arrested, he told Peter to listen for a cockerel crowing. He told us that God is so loving he even knows when a sparrow dies. And he said that if anyone didn't want to hear about God, it was like giving your best pearls to a pig!

Camels, sheep, goats, donkeys, cockerels, sparrows and pigs. All these animals were part of Jesus' daily life. But sadly not penguins.

NOW LOOK AT:

Did Jesus go to school? p21
What sort of stories did Jesus tell? p63
Why did Jesus use stories to tell people about God? p68
Did Jesus draw cartoons? p70

What jobs did people do?

Just like today, a whole range of skills were used in Jesus' time to make the things that people needed. As well as the fishermen, farmers and carpenters there were many people who worked with their hands.

Potters made jars and pots from clay. Sitting on a stone seat, they used their feet to turn a large wheel. As the clay turned on the wheel, they shaped the clay into pots with their hands.

Masons worked with stone. They carved stones for building rich peoples' houses. They cut tombs out of rock. They cut deep wells into stone, to catch rainwater.

Smiths made tools and weapons out of metal. The metal would be melted in a hot furnace, then shaped into whatever people might need: ploughs for farmers, tools for carpenters, arrow-tips and spears for soldiers.

Tanners made things out of leather (the skin of oxen, sheep or goats), such as sandals, wineskins or harness for oxen. Tanning was a dirty, smelly job and so tanners worked well away from other people, and near lots of water so they could wash off the smell!

NOW LOOK AT:

Did people grow their own food? p39

Was being a shepherd a good job? p41

Why did people hate tax collectors? p31

What was Jesus' house like? p23

What did Jesus tell people about God?

Jesus said that God is closer than we think. If a person turns away from things they know are wrong, then they can know God's love. This is good news for everyone.

Jesus taught the secret of true happiness. He said that truly happy people are people who know they need God. Truly happy people work for peace, are "pure in heart", and humble. Their greatest desire is to do what God wants.

Jesus taught that God is kind, generous and loving. He told a story about a man giving a great feast. The man sent his servants out to invite people to the feast. Lots of them didn't want to come. But the man sent out his servants again and again, looking for people who were poor and hungry and lonely, until his house was full of people enjoying the feast.

In just the same way, said Jesus, lots of people don't want to know about God. But he will not rest until everyone who wants to know him has met him for themselves.

NOW LOOK AT:

How does God feel about us? p50

What is the Lord's prayer? p57

What did Jesus teach about prayer? p30

How did Jesus know that God was his Father? p24

Did people grow their own food?

Every family had at least a little bit of land to grow some food. It was very important to look after your crops. There were no supermarkets or freezers, so everything was eaten in season, or stored by drying or salting.

Farmers grew grain (for bread), vines, olives, vegetables, figs, dates and other fruits. Flax was grown to make linen for clothing. Some parts of Israel were very fertile but other parts were dry and rocky and depended on getting enough rain each year.

There were no tractors or machines. Farmers usually had one or two oxen to pull the plough. They were yoked to the plough, and as the oxen pulled forward, the farmer pressed the blade into the earth.

The corn was sown by hand: the farmer carried a big bag of corn and scattered it over the ground. Once the corn had grown, it was cut with a moon-shaped blade called a sickle. The good corn would be stored in barns.

NOW LOOK AT:

Why did people hate tax collectors? p31

What was the weather like where Jesus lived? p27

Where did Jesus grow up? p18

What did Jesus eat? p29

Why did Jesus come into our world?

Jesus was baptised when he was thirty. Soon afterwards he went to a synagogue, just as he had done all his life. It was his turn to read from the Scriptures (holy writings of the Jewish people). He read a passage from the prophet Isaiah, which had been written hundreds of years before. It was about God's promised Messiah who would:

Bring good news to the poor... Jesus told people how much God loved them. Jesus said that everyone matters to God, however poor or weak or insignificant.

Make blind people see... Jesus went around healing people who were ill. He also helped people to "see" the truth about God.

Set free those people who were treated badly or weighed down with unhappiness.

This is the "work" that Jesus had come to do. He had come to show people a new way of living, with God in the centre of their lives.

NOW LOOK AT:

How do we know Jesus isn't just a story? p16
What did Jesus teach about poor people? p55
What did Jesus teach about love? p51
Why did Jesus make sick people well? p71

Was being a shepherd a good job?

In the time of Jesus, being a shepherd was a dangerous occupation. The shepherd's job was to make sure that none of his sheep were stolen or attacked by wild animals.

The land was dry and rocky and there wasn't much grass and so the shepherd had to lead his sheep to the best grazing land. This could be miles from home. Shepherds often built pens or 'folds' to keep their sheep safe at night. This would be a circle of stones, with an opening for the sheep to go in. Instead of a gate, the shepherd slept across the opening. The sheep knew their own shepherd so well that they recognised his voice.

Jesus said that he was like a shepherd because he cared so much for people. He told a story about a shepherd who lost one of his hundred sheep. He left the ninety-nine and searched for the lost sheep until he found it. Jesus told this story to show that every one of us is important to God.

NOW LOOK AT:

Who were the first people to visit baby Jesus? p10
How does God feel about us? p50
What was it like being a fisherman? p48
What sort of stories did Jesus tell? p63

Did Jesus own a Bible?

No. In fact, in the time of Jesus only very rich people owned books. That's because books were much harder to make in those days. They didn't have paper. And they didn't have printing.

Instead of paper, people used something called "papyrus". Papyrus was made out of bulrushes. Thin strips of bulrush pith would be laid side by side, then soaked in river water and glue. They would then be beaten with a mallet and smoothed with a rough stone.

The papyrus would then be dried and rolled up into a scroll, and someone would write the book on it by hand: a long and expensive process!

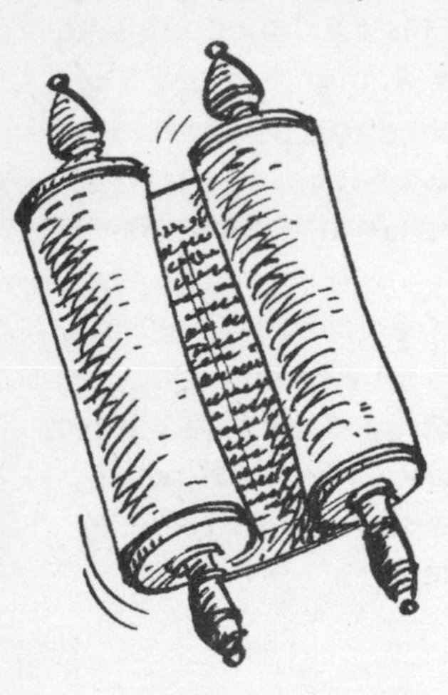

So Jesus didn't own his own Bible. He got to know the Old Testament by reading the scrolls kept in the synagogue. The Old Testament was written in a language called Hebrew (an older form of Aramaic – the language Jesus spoke). It contains lots of different kinds of writing: history (the story of God's people), prophecy (God's message to his people), and wisdom (wise sayings written down).

NOW LOOK AT:

What language did Jesus speak? p26

Did Jesus go to church? p19

Did Jesus write any books? p47

How did Jesus travel? p35

Were there doctors?

Every town was supposed to have a doctor (for medicine) and a surgeon (for operations). Some of them were very good. One historical record says that a man was shot through the lungs with an arrow. Doctors removed the arrow and he recovered.

Luke, the Gospel-writer, was a doctor. He also wrote the Acts of the Apostles.

It seems, though, that many people didn't really trust doctors. One woman healed by Jesus had "spent all she had on doctors... but got worse". Another proverb said that 'even the best doctor deserved to go to hell.' That may have been because lots of them made up 'cures' to sell which did no good.

It may also have been because there were no anaesthetics and few pain-killers. Advice to a surgeon from the time of Jesus was to try and blot out the screams of the person being operated on. The pain relief used most frequently was a drink of wine mixed with herbs. This deadened pain and was sometimes given to criminals before they were crucified.

NOW LOOK AT:

What happened when someone died? p44

What happened when Jesus healed people? p46

Why did Jesus make sick people well? p71

How did Jesus die? p84

see John chapter 19, verses 28–42 and chapter 20, verses 1–9

What happened when someone died?

In the Jewish culture there were traditional customs for burial and for mourning. When someone died, the body was first of all washed and then special oils and spices were rubbed onto it. The body was then wrapped in white "grave clothes".

Before the body was buried, lots of people gathered round to mourn. Some were members of the dead person's family. Others were "professional" mourners, paid to come and grieve. They wailed loudly, tore their clothes and put ash on their heads.

Because it was a hot country, people were often buried on the same day they died. The soil wasn't very deep, so people were often buried in caves or prepared tombs, cut out of rock. A large boulder was placed at the mouth of the cave to keep out jackals.

Jesus' body was buried in a cave. When his friends saw the boulder rolled away from the cave entrance, it was the first sign that God had raised Jesus from the dead.

NOW LOOK AT:

Did Jesus know he was going to die? p77
What happened at the first Easter? p86
How do we know that Jesus rose from the dead? p91
What were weddings like in Jesus' day? p34

Did Jesus have an ordinary job?

Jesus was a carpenter – someone skilled at making things out of wood. Joseph – the man who brought Jesus up – was a carpenter too. When he was a child, Jesus probably watched Joseph at work and learned from him everything a carpenter needs to know.

Carpenters made all kinds of things for people in their village. If you were building a new house, the carpenter would make roof beams, door frames and window fittings. If you'd already built your house and needed furniture, the carpenter would make you beds, chairs, and tables. If you were a farmer, you'd go to the carpenter for ploughs and yokes (wooden bars to join two oxen together so they could plough).

There was no electricity in those days, of course, so it's likely that Jesus was a strong man, using his own muscle-power to work his tools: chisel, mallet, and hand-drill.

For most of his life, until he was about thirty, Jesus earned his living as a carpenter, taking rough bits of wood and turning them into something beautiful and useful.

NOW LOOK AT:

Why did Jesus come into our world?	p40
What jobs did people do?	p37
Who were Jesus' parents?	p17
What happened when Jesus was baptised?	p28

see Luke chapter 7, verses 18–23

What happened when Jesus healed people?

When John the Baptist was in prison, he sent his friends to see what Jesus was doing. Jesus told them to go back and tell John everything that he was doing: blind people could see again, disabled people could walk again, deaf people could hear again.

For Jesus, these were signs of God's power and God's love. When he healed people, Jesus showed that God really loved them. But he often told people not to tell anyone what had happened. That's because he didn't want anyone to follow him just because they saw exciting things.

Sometimes people asked Jesus to do a miracle because they didn't believe in him. They wanted him to prove that he was God's Son. Jesus always refused to do miracles for people like that. He knew that even when that sort of person saw miracles, they still wouldn't believe.

So when Jesus healed people, it was because he loved them and wanted to make them better.

NOW LOOK AT:

Why did Jesus make sick people well?	*p71*
Why did Jesus come into our world?	*p40*
Were there doctors?	*p43*
Is Jesus God's Son?	*p15*

see John chapter 21, verses 24,25

Did Jesus write any books?

No. Although the things Jesus did and said changed the world, he didn't write a single book. But Jesus' friends remembered what he did and said and told other people, to make sure they didn't forget.

In the end, Jesus' friends knew that those things were so important that they wrote them down in the four books we call the "Gospels". The four Gospels are called "Matthew", "Mark", "Luke" and "John", after the names of the men who wrote them. "Mark" was probably written about thirty years after Jesus died.

The four Gospels are like Jesus' life story. They tell us what Jesus said and did, where he was born and where he grew up, how he lived and how he died, and how he was raised from the dead.

Jesus may not have written any books, but at the end of John's Gospel, the writer says that if absolutely everything Jesus did was written down, there wouldn't be room in the world for all the books that would be written!

NOW LOOK AT:

How did Jesus die? p84
What did Jesus say about human beings? p66
Why did Jesus use stories to tell people about God? p68
Did Jesus draw cartoons? p70

What was it like being a fisherman?

For much of his life, Jesus lived and worked near Lake Galilee – a very large lake – where he met many fishermen, including four of his disciples. Peter, Andrew, James and John all made their living by fishing before Jesus met them.

There were two kinds of fishing in Jesus' day: fishing from a boat, or fishing from the shore. If you fished from a boat you would use a drag-net and could sometimes catch huge numbers of fish. Fishing could be dangerous: sometimes fierce storms blew up on Lake Galilee without any warning.

If you fished from the shore you would use a hand-net. You would throw it into the shallow water and pull it back to the shore.

After a long night's fishing, the fishermen would sort out their catch. Any fish that were too small, or not good to eat, were thrown back into the water. The rest were taken to market. The ones which weren't eaten fresh were dried and salted to preserve them.

Once they had sorted their catch, the fishermen would wash and mend their nets, or repair their boats and sails.

NOW LOOK AT:

What did Jesus teach about poor people? p55
Did people grow their own food? p39
How did Jesus travel? p35

Did Jesus mind what people thought of him?

In Jericho there lived a man called Zacchaeus. The people of Jericho hated Zacchaeus because he was a despised tax collector. They hated him because they were sure he cheated them out of lots of money.

One day Jesus came to Jericho. A huge crowd turned out to welcome him. Everyone wanted to invite him to their house for a meal. But Jesus chose to go to Zacchaeus' house.

Everyone grumbled and complained, because they thought that Zacchaeus wasn't good enough for Jesus. But Jesus was a strong person who wanted to do what was right, and on this occasion it meant showing love to someone everybody hated. After Jesus' visit, Zacchaeus changed his ways and stopped cheating people.

Another time, a tax collector called Levi invited Jesus to a huge party. Jesus knew that lots of "bad" people would be there. He knew that his enemies would be offended if he went. But he didn't care. Bad or not, they were people God loved. Jesus gladly went to Levi's house even though other people thought he shouldn't.

NOW LOOK AT:

Why did people hate tax collectors? p31

What did Jesus teach about love? p51

Who made Jesus angry? p73

Who said Jesus had to die? p82

How does God feel about us?

Jesus told a story about a man with two sons: one of them asked for his share of his father's money which he would get after his father died. He left home and wasted the money on parties. When his money ran out, he got a job looking after pigs – the worst kind of job in those days. One day he was so hungry he nearly had to eat the pigs' food. So he decided to go home, say "sorry" to his dad, and offer to be his dad's slave.

When he was nearly home, his father saw him. He ran down the road and hugged him. He welcomed him right back into the family, and they had a huge party. The other brother was jealous, but the father reminded him that he was loved just as much as the other son.

Jesus told that story to show us what God is like – always loving and forgiving, like the best kind of father. That means...

* All his children are special to him.
* He knows what we need before we ask him.
* He is angry when one of his children hurts another.
* He is always ready to forgive us.
* He loves us more than we can imagine.

NOW LOOK AT:

What is the most important rule to live by? p56

Is Jesus God's Son? p15

What is the Lord's prayer? p57

Why did Jesus use stories to tell people about God? p68

What did Jesus teach about love?

Someone once asked Jesus which was the most important of God's rules. "Love God as much as you can," he replied, "and love other people as much as you love yourself."

This means some very important and difficult things: we have to be kind even to people we don't like. Jesus taught us to love even our enemies. That's why he prayed for the Roman soldiers who were nailing him to the cross.

It means not just saying things, but doing things. Jesus didn't just say he loved his friends, he did things to show how much he loved them. On the night before he died, he washed his friends' hot and tired feet – a job which was usually done by a servant.

It means thinking about how you like to be treated, and then treating people in the same way. This is called Jesus' "Golden Rule". It is written down in the Bible like this: "Do for others what you would like them to do for you."

NOW LOOK AT:

Why did Jesus make sick people well? p71

What is a Good Samaritan? p61

Who were Jesus' enemies? p72

Did Jesus get bullied? p83

Why did Jesus break other people's rules?

At the time of Jesus, some of the religious groups, like Pharisees, had lots of rules about how people should behave. Jesus broke these rules when it seemed that the rules had become more important than people.

The Sabbath was originally given by God to be a day of rest. But religious people had made lots of extra rules about having a rest, and there were long lists of what you couldn't do on the Sabbath. The list included "sewing two stitches...writing two letters...and tying a knot."

Jesus could see that some people thought the rules were more important than God. So one Sabbath day he broke their rules on purpose. With lots of people there, and with his enemies watching, he healed a man who had a paralysed hand. He knew that according to the Pharisees' rules he wasn't supposed to heal him, because it was the Sabbath. He healed him anyway... because to Jesus, people matter more than rules. And his enemies went out and planned to kill him.

NOW LOOK AT:

What did Jesus teach about love? p51
What is the most important rule to live by? p56
Did Jesus do anything wrong? p75
Who were Jesus' enemies? p72

What did Jesus teach about forgiveness?

Jesus told a story about a king. One of his servants owed him lots of money. He couldn't pay, so the king ordered the servant to go to prison.

When the servant pleaded with the king, the king changed his mind. He let the servant off. He didn't have to pay anything!

It's a story about God forgiving us. We do wrong things. But when we say we are sorry, God says, "OK, let's forget about what you've done. You can have a new start." – just like the king said to the servant.

But the story continued. The servant, who had been let off all that money, bumped into someone who owed him some money – a tiny amount. He couldn't pay, and although he begged for mercy, the servant threw him into prison.

The king found out about it and was very angry. The servant had been let off so much; he should have treated the other person in the same way.

It's just like that with us, says Jesus. God has forgiven us so much. We should forgive people who do wrong to us.

NOW LOOK AT:

How does God feel about us?	*p50*
Why did the wise man build his house upon the rock?	*p62*
Did Jesus get bullied?	*p83*
Why did Jesus have to die?	*p85*

Did Jesus pay taxes?

Jesus lived in an occupied country: the Romans ruled the land of Israel and everyone had to pay their taxes to the Romans. Naturally, the Jewish people did not like paying these taxes.

Once, Jesus' enemies asked him if Jews should pay taxes to Rome. It was a trick question. If Jesus said "Yes," he would have angered people who hated paying it. If Jesus said "No," his enemies could have handed him over to the Romans as a trouble-maker.

By way of a reply, Jesus asked to see a Roman coin. On it was a picture of Caesar, with some words that claimed he was a god! No wonder people hated paying these taxes.

Then Jesus simply said: "Give to Caesar what is Caesar's, and to God what is God's." It was a brilliant answer. He was saying: "Pay your taxes gladly... the money is spent on good things, like decent roads and clean water." But he was also saying, "Give a little bit of your money to Rome... but give all of yourself to God."

NOW LOOK AT:

Where was Jesus born? p9
Why did people hate tax collectors? p31
What did Jesus teach about money? p58
What sort of money did Jesus use? p60

see Luke chapter 18, verses 18–27

What did Jesus teach about poor people?

There have always been poor people. But Jesus wanted his followers to do something for them.

He told a rich young man to go and sell everything he had and then give the money to the poor. The rich man wouldn't do it, and went away sad.

He told a story about himself as a king, separating good people from bad. The good people had given food to hungry people and drink to thirsty people. They had given clothes to people who needed them, and had looked after poorly people. The bad people had done none of these things. To the good people the King said, "Come!" To the bad people he said, "Away from me!"

Jesus told another story. There was a rich man. At his gate lay a beggar called Lazarus. The rich man gave nothing to the beggar. Then both men died. The beggar, Lazarus, was taken to heaven. The rich man was not.

In these ways, and in others, Jesus asked people who were not poor to look after people who were.

NOW LOOK AT:

What is a Good Samaritan? p61

Why did Jesus break other people's rules? p52

Who were the first people to visit the baby Jesus? p10

What did Jesus teach about love? p51

What is the most important rule to live by?

One day someone came up to Jesus. He asked Jesus to think about all the rules and commands that God had given his people. He wanted to know which one Jesus thought was most important.

Jesus couldn't give just one. He gave two. He said the most important rule was to love God with all our heart, mind, soul and strength. He said the second most important rule was to love other people as much as we love ourselves.

Just two rules! And if you think about it, they're the only rules we need. Just think what a great place the world would be if everyone loved God, and everyone loved each other.

When Jesus talked about "love" he wasn't just talking about a nice feeling. He was talking about putting God and other people first. And if only we all did that, the world would be a better place to live in.

What is the Lord's prayer?

Jesus' friends asked him to teach them to pray. He taught them to pray using what we now call "The Lord's Prayer".

It starts with the words **Our Father**. Jesus reminds us that we're praying to our Father God, who loves us perfectly – even better than the very best of good fathers.

We go on to ask **hallowed be your name**. That means that we ask for people to treat God with great respect.

Then we ask **your kingdom come, your will be done**. Often human beings ignore God, and his world is filled with badness: war, greed, unfairness. Jesus taught us to pray for the world to be as God wants it to be.

Then Jesus taught us to pray for ourselves: **give us today our daily bread**. We ask for God to give us what we need to stay alive.

Next, we ask God to **forgive us our sins**, but for that to happen we need to **forgive those who sin against us**.

Lastly, we ask God to keep us safe from anything that might take us away from him: **lead us not into temptation, but deliver us from evil**.

NOW LOOK AT:

When did Jesus pray? p59

How does God feel about us? p50

Did Jesus go to church? p19

What did Jesus teach about forgiveness? p53

see Matthew chapter 19, verses 19–21

What did Jesus teach about money?

In some ways, the world hasn't changed much since the time of Jesus. Just like today, lots of people thought that money was the most important thing in life and spent their lives trying to get more and more.

Jesus felt sorry for people who lived like that. He could see that having lots of money often made them worried because it was never enough. In running after money, people missed out on other things. Jesus said that what really makes people happy is giving things away, not getting more and more.

Jesus did not hate money, and he showed people that it is something they can use – to help other people. Jesus once told a rich young man to sell everything he had and give all his money to the poor.

Of course Jesus understands that we need enough to live on. But he taught us not to be worried about that. He taught us to trust God to look after us because he knows what we need.

NOW LOOK AT:

What sort of money did Jesus use?	*p60*
Why did Jesus get angry in the temple?	*p33*
Did Jesus pay taxes?	*p54*
Who were Jesus' enemies?	*p72*

When did Jesus pray?

Because Jesus was God's Son, and because he loved his Father deeply, talking to God in prayer was very important to him.

Jesus would get up very early, while it was still dark. He would leave his house and find a quiet place to be alone where no one could disturb him. That way, he had time to be close to God before the day started.

Jesus prayed when he needed God to help him make decisions. When he was going to choose just twelve men to be his "disciples", he spent all night praying about it!

Jesus prayed when he needed God's strength. The night before he died, he was frightened. He asked God if he really had to be nailed to a cross and die. But he went on to pray, "Your will be done." Jesus always wanted to do what his Father wanted him to do. So he prayed whenever he wanted to be close to God.

NOW LOOK AT:

What did Jesus teach about prayer?	*p30*
Could Jesus pray anywhere?	*p64*
Was Jesus ever afraid?	*p74*
What is the Lord's prayer?	*p57*

What sort of money did Jesus use?

If you travelled back in time to Jesus' world, you would find that there were all kinds of coins around: some very valuable... others not at all.

The most valuable amount of money Jesus mentions is the silver **talent**. Jesus told a story about a man going on a journey. He gave one of his servants five talents to look after. That was a lot of money!

Next down is the **stater**. When Judas led Jesus' enemies to him, they gave Judas thirty staters. The stater was a silver coin, but worth much less than the talent.

Still silver, and smaller again, was the **drachma**. Jesus told a story about a poor woman who lost a drachma. She was so pleased when she found it again that she had a party!

Next came the copper coins. The copper **assarion** could buy you two sparrows... if you really wanted two sparrows!

And last of all came the **lepton**. "Lepton" means "small" or "thin". Jesus watched a poor widow put her last "lepton" into the collection box at the temple. He pointed out to his disciples that she had given everything she had to live on.

NOW LOOK AT:

What happened in the week before Jesus died? p79

Did Jesus pay taxes? p54

What did Jesus teach about money? p58

see Luke chapter 10, verses 25–37

What is a Good Samaritan?

The people who lived in Jesus' country were called "Jews". The people who lived in the country to the North (Samaria) were called "Samaritans".

In the time of Jesus, the Jews hated the Samaritans. The Samaritans hated the Jews as well. When Jesus was a boy some Samaritans had insulted the Jews by scattering dead men's bones in the temple in Jerusalem.

But Jesus told the Jews a story about a "Good Samaritan". A man is travelling from Jerusalem to Jericho. Thieves attack him. They strip him and leave him half dead.

A priest goes by. He does nothing to help the man. A Levite – one of the top religious people – goes by. He too does nothing. Then a Samaritan comes along. The Jew would have been shocked to hear Jesus say that the Samaritan was the one who helped the robbed man.

So a Good Samaritan is someone who goes out of their way to help somebody else. Jesus told the story to show that love isn't just a feeling – it's actually doing something to help. He told the story to show that we shouldn't help only our friends, but even people we don't actually like.

NOW LOOK AT:

Where was Jesus born?	*p9*
What is the most important rule to live by?	*p56*
What did Jesus teach about love?	*p51*
What did Jesus teach about forgiveness?	*p53*

Why did the wise man build his house upon the rock?

Jesus told a story about two men. They both wanted to build a house. One of the men was wise. He decided to build his house on rock. After all, when storms blow up, your house needs to be as strong as possible.

The other man was stupid. He thought that all this rock business was too much like hard work. He built his house in the first place he could find – which just happened to be on some soft sand.

Well, a storm did blow up. And the house on the rock was fine, even though the wind howled around it. The house on the sand, though, collapsed in a heap and left the stupid man out in the cold.

It's a story about how we listen to Jesus. If we hear what Jesus has to say and do it, we're like wise people building on a solid foundation. If we hear what Jesus has to say and ignore it, we're just like the lazy man who built his house on sand.

NOW LOOK AT:

How do I find out more about Jesus? p92
How do we know Jesus isn't just a story? p16
What was the weather like where Jesus lived? p27
Why did Jesus use stories to tell people about God? p68

see Matthew chapter 13, verse 44

What sort of stories did Jesus tell?

Jesus wanted people to understand about God and what he was like. So he told stories about everyday things. Lots of these stories are recorded in the Gospels. Some of them are about a man building a house, a farmer sowing seeds and a woman losing some money.

Some of Jesus' stories are very short: he said that knowing God was like a man finding buried treasure in a field.

Other stories are quite long: like the story he told about a man who had two sons. This story shows that God is a loving Father.

Some of Jesus' stories are more like riddles: he said that the way God worked in the world was like yeast working its way through dough (work out what that means).

Other stories mean just one thing – like a story he told about a king who forgave his servant who was in debt.

Some of Jesus' stories could means lots of things – like a story he told about people working all day in a vineyard. Some people worked all day... others worked the last hour... but they all got the same pay. What do you think that means? You can read the whole story for yourself in Matthew chapter 20, verses 1–16.

NOW LOOK AT:

Why did Jesus use stories to tell people about God?	*p68*
How does God feel about us?	*p50*
What did Jesus teach about forgiveness?	*p53*
Did Jesus draw cartoons?	*p70*

Could Jesus pray anywhere?

Jesus sometimes met very "religious" people who liked showing off. These people liked to pray standing on street corners so that passers-by would see them and think they were really good.

Jesus told his followers how to pray: "Go into your room, shut the door, and pray to our Father." He told them not to "babble" on, because God knows what each person needs.

But that doesn't mean that Jesus only ever prayed indoors. He was so sure that God loved him that he was happy to talk to God anywhere.

He prayed by the river after he was baptised; on a mountain top with his friends; in the quietness of the hills in the early morning.

He prayed when he healed people, and he prayed the night before he died in the Garden of Gethsemane.

For Jesus, talking to God was so important that any time, and any place, would do.

NOW LOOK AT:

Who baptised Jesus? p22
What did Jesus do on the night before he died? p80
Did Jesus go to church? p19
When did Jesus pray? p59

see Luke chapter 14, verses 16–24

What did Jesus teach about heaven?

Whenever Jesus wanted to talk about what heaven was like, he talked about parties: "Heaven's like a fantastic wedding reception... it's like a great feast... like an enormous banquet." What's more, Jesus said that God wants everyone to be there. Jesus told a story about heaven. It was like a man throwing a big party. The man invited lots of people, but they didn't want to come. So he sent out his servants to invite other people, saying, "I want my house to be full!"

But Jesus also said that not everyone will be in heaven. He told another story, about a rich man. The rich man ignored a poor beggar at his gate. After they both died, the poor beggar went to heaven. The rich man did not.

Jesus told people to make sure they're not left out. He said that the way to heaven is like a door that's still open, but one day it's going to shut. We go through the door by becoming God's friends, asking him to forgive us the wrong things we've done, and asking him to help us live as followers of Jesus.

NOW LOOK AT:

see Matthew chapter 6, verses 31–34

What did Jesus say about human beings?

Jesus had some hard words about human beings. He knows what we are like. He said that from inside come all kinds of nasty things: bad thoughts, stealing, murder, being greedy, being jealous...

But Jesus didn't leave it there. He went on to say that, even though we often do wrong things, each human being is very special to God. God loves each one and he wants to forgive us and give us a new start.

Jesus told people that God is always looking after them. He never stops loving the people he has made.

Because God loves us that much, Jesus said we should not spend our days worrying about our own lives. After all, God knows that we need food, drink and clothes. He will make sure that we are cared for.

Jesus said that the most important thing for any human being is to try their hardest to live in a way that pleases God.

NOW LOOK AT:

Did Jesus do anything wrong? p75
What is the most important rule to live by? p56
Why did Jesus get angry in the temple? p33
How does God feel about us? p50

Why did Jesus think that children were important?

Just like today, in Jesus' time there were some grown-ups who ignored children, or who thought children were not worth bothering about or that they got in the way.

One day some parents brought their little children to Jesus. They wanted him to hold their children and say a prayer for God's blessing.

Some of Jesus' friends were annoyed. They wanted to send the children away. Perhaps they thought the children were too unimportant for Jesus, or that they might get in the way of Jesus' work.

But for Jesus, no one was unimportant. Everyone mattered to him, and especially children. If children felt they were unimportant to some people, he made sure they knew they were important to him. So he gave the children a hug, and asked God to look after them and be with them.

NOW LOOK AT:

Did Jesus get bullied? p83

What did Jesus teach about poor people? p55

Did Jesus have brothers and sisters? p20

How did Jesus know that God was his Father? p24

Why did Jesus use stories to tell people about God?

Think of your favourite TV programme. Then imagine if the TV went off halfway through. You'd really want to know what happened next!

That's partly why Jesus told stories, sometimes called parables. Everyone loves a good story. You get drawn into it and you want to know what happens next. Afterwards, a story sticks in your mind.

But with some of the stories, there was more to it than that. Sometimes it was a way of finding people who really wanted to know about God.

How did it work? Well, Jesus would tell a story and not explain what it meant. If people listened to the story and then drifted off, they showed they weren't really all that interested.

But if they really wanted to know, they waited behind afterwards, or they found Jesus in a quiet corner. When they asked what the story meant they showed that they really wanted to understand. So Jesus then explained to them the hidden meaning in the story.

NOW LOOK AT:

How does God feel about us? p50
Is Jesus God's Son? p15
Why did the wise man build his house upon the rock? p62
What sort of stories did Jesus tell? p63

Was Jesus ever sad?

Jesus was sad when his friend Lazarus died. Jesus went to his funeral. Lazarus' sisters and friends were all crying. Jesus wept with them. He was sad that people die.

Jesus was sad when he visited Jerusalem, the capital city of his country. He knew that one day the Romans would destroy the city and even kill the children. And he was sad because God's people wouldn't hear his message.

Jesus was sad when he saw and heard of the bad things people did – to themselves and to each other. He was sad when they did not listen to his message about how they could start a new life with God.

But even though Jesus himself was sad, he didn't want people to feel sorry for him. When he was carrying his wooden cross to the place where he was going to be killed, lots of people followed him, crying. Jesus told them not to weep for him, but for themselves. He knew that when Jerusalem was destroyed it would be terrible for them.

NOW LOOK AT:

Who made Jesus angry? p73

Did Jesus know he was going to die? p77

Was Jesus ever afraid? p74

Did Jesus get bullied? p83

Did Jesus draw cartoons?

He didn't draw cartoons with a pen. But he often did with his words.

For example, he thought of people who find fault with other people, but never think they might be the one to blame. You might know someone like that – they always want other people to change but never think of changing themselves.

Jesus said they're like someone trying to take a speck of dust out of someone's eye... when all the time they've got a plank in their own! They should deal with their own problem first before picking on anyone else.

Then there are people who make a fuss about little things but ignore important things – like people who complain about not being able to get their favourite breakfast cereal at their local supermarket but who do nothing to help all the starving children in the world. He said they're like people with a fly... and a camel in their soup. They carefully take out the fly, but swallow the camel whole!

NOW LOOK AT:

Did Jesus write any books? p47

Why did Jesus use stories to tell people about God? p68

Why did Jesus make sick people well?

One day a man came to Jesus. He was suffering from a horrible skin disease. He begged Jesus to make him better. Jesus looked at the man. He was filled with pity. He stretched out his hand and touched him. Immediately the man was healed.

That's not the only time the Bible tells us about Jesus making sick people well. Lots of people were healed by Jesus – children, adults, Romans, Jews, rich people, poor people. Some of them had been born with an illness, others had recently become sick. But each one of them met Jesus who made them better.

Why did Jesus do it? First, because he is God's Son and has God's power. Second, because Jesus loves people. He couldn't bear to see people suffer.

NOW LOOK AT:

What is the most important rule to live by? p56

What happened when Jesus healed people? p46

What is a Good Samaritan? p61

Why did Jesus have to die? p85

Who were Jesus' enemies?

Jesus had many powerful enemies, who plotted his death. On the one hand were the Sadducees (*Sad-you-sees*). On the other, the Pharisees (*Fa-ri-sees*).

The Sadducees were wealthy, upper-class people. They controlled the temple in Jerusalem. They were powerful because they worked closely with the Romans, who ruled Jesus' country.

Because they were well off, the Sadducees didn't want things to change. They especially didn't like Jesus' new teaching about life after death. Because they were in charge of the temple, they were angry when Jesus threw the market traders out of it.

The Pharisees took all the rules of religion very seriously. As well as the rules God gave to his people (like the Ten Commandments), they made up rules of their own. They looked down on people who didn't keep their religious rules.

Jesus often clashed with the Pharisees. For Jesus, religion was not about keeping lots of rules. It was about knowing God and realising that he loves us. Jesus deliberately broke the Pharisees' rules and the Pharisees plotted to kill Jesus.

NOW LOOK AT:

Who were Jesus' friends? p25

Why did Jesus get angry in the temple? p33

What happened in the week before Jesus died? p79

Did Jesus get bullied? p83

Who made Jesus angry?

Jesus was angry with people who pretend. He met lots of people who pretended to be nice. He knew they weren't really like that. So he called them "whitewashed tombs": on the outside they looked good, but inside they were full of bad things like greed and jealousy.

Jesus preferred people who were honest about what they were really like: people who asked God to help them.

Jesus was angry with people who made a big show about being religious: people who liked to be seen praying; people who liked to be seen giving money to God. He preferred people who didn't show off: people who prayed quietly on their own and gave money secretly.

Jesus was angry with people who made a big fuss about keeping little rules but did nothing about the really big things. For example, there were people who carefully gave God a tenth of their spices, but gave nothing to poor people. He called his followers to serve the poor and to work for a fairer world.

NOW LOOK AT:

How did Jesus die?	*p84*
Why did Jesus think that children were important?	*p67*
What is a Christian?	*p89*
Why did Jesus get angry in the temple?	*p33*

Was Jesus ever afraid?

Jesus was not afraid when people hated him. The people of his home town of Nazareth didn't like the message he brought about God. This didn't stop Jesus talking about God, even though they tried to kill him.

Jesus was not afraid of powerful enemies. Many times he knew they were watching him, trying to get him to do something wrong. When he healed someone on the Sabbath day, his enemies plotted to kill him.

Jesus was not afraid of terrible storms. He was once in a boat on the Sea of Galilee. A storm blew up, and Jesus' friends were terrified. But Jesus told the waves to be still, and immediately the sea was calm. Jesus asked his friends, "Why were you frightened?"

But there was one time, the night before he died, that he was frightened.

It was the dead of night and he was praying in a garden. He knew his enemies were coming to get him. He knew they would kill him. It was an awful thought, and he asked God if it really had to happen.

Even though he was frightened, Jesus showed great courage. He didn't run away. He waited for his enemies to come.

NOW LOOK AT:

What happened when Jesus was arrested?	*p81*
What was the weather like where Jesus lived?	*p27*
Who made Jesus angry?	*p73*

Did Jesus do anything wrong?

After Jesus was baptised, he went into the desert. He was there for forty days, thinking about the kind of things God wanted him to do.

In the desert, God's enemy, sometimes called the devil, tried to get Jesus to do wrong. He tried to get Jesus to use his power to turn stones into bread because he was hungry. This was a temptation for Jesus, because he could have done it, but he wanted to rely on God.

Then God's enemy tried to get Jesus to use his power to impress people by throwing himself off a high building and letting angels catch him before he hit the ground.

The devil even tried to get Jesus to worship him. But Jesus was strong. He refused to do what the devil wanted him to. He only wanted to do what God wanted.

Jesus resisted temptations all through his life, and he never gave in to them. At his trial, when his enemies wanted to kill him, they had to make up lies about bad things he had done. Even his judge said he had done nothing wrong. But he still said Jesus had to die.

NOW LOOK AT:

Did Jesus mind what people thought of him? p49

How did Jesus die? p84

Who baptised Jesus? p22

Why did Jesus have to die? p85

Did Jesus ever get tired?

Just like you or me, Jesus got tired when working hard, or after a long journey. In those days, people travelled everywhere on foot so it's not surprising that Jesus got tired. After all, he went to lots of different places.

In fact, Jesus was once so tired that although he was on a boat, and the boat was in a storm, and his friends were scared stiff... he was fast asleep in the back of the boat.

And Jesus also felt a different kind of tiredness. One day, a woman who had been ill for a long time touched the hem of Jesus' cloak. She thought he would not notice because of the crowds but Jesus felt the power going out of him to heal her. Wherever he went, crowds of people flocked after him, asking him to make them better.

Sometimes, Jesus just got tired of people's lack of belief in God. Once, a father brought his son to Jesus' disciples. They could not heal him, and Jesus said, "How long have I got to put up with you?"!

NOW LOOK AT:

What happened when Jesus healed people? p46
Where did Jesus grow up? p18
How did Jesus travel? p35
Why did Jesus ride a donkey? p78

see Mark chapter 12, verses 1–8

Did Jesus know he was going to die?

Yes. Towards the end of his life on earth, Jesus told his friends several times that he would be killed in Jerusalem. Jesus told them he had to die, because it was part of God's plan.

Then, during the week before he died, Jesus told a powerful story. In the story a man planted a vineyard, and left servants to look after it.

The owner of the vineyard sent a number of messengers to ask for his share of the grapes. But the servants beat up the messengers and killed them. At last the man sent his only son. But when the servants saw him coming, they killed him, hoping to get the vineyard for themselves.

It's a story with a meaning. The man who planted the vineyard is God. The vineyard is the world, and the servants are humankind.

When the man asks for grapes it's like God asking us to live as he wants us to. But we refuse. When finally the man's son comes, he is killed, just like Jesus was killed on the cross.

NOW LOOK AT:

Was Jesus a real person? p14

Who said Jesus had to die? p82

How did Jesus die? p84

What did Jesus do on the night before he died? p80

Why did Jesus ride a donkey?

For hundreds of years before Jesus was born, God's people had been waiting for a special king. This king was going to come into Jerusalem "humble and riding on a donkey".

Those words came true a few days before Jesus died. He had travelled on foot to Jerusalem and arrived at the Mount of Olives, a hillside looking down over the city.

He sent two of his friends to a village nearby. They found a donkey and brought it to Jesus. They spread their clothes on the donkey's back, like a saddle, and Jesus got on. Then he rode on the donkey into the city. He wanted to show people that he was the special king. And riding a donkey was a sign that the king was coming in peace.

A crowd of people saw him and became very excited. They spread clothes and palm leaves on the road to welcome the special king. They began to shout, "Hosanna!" which means "Save us!" And when others asked "Who is this?" the crowd said, "This is Jesus, the prophet from Nazareth!"

NOW LOOK AT:

Who were the Wise Men?	*p11*
What did Jesus do on the night before he died?	*p80*
Where did Jesus grow up?	*p18*
Did Jesus ever see a penguin?	*p36*

What happened in the week before Jesus died?

When Jesus got angry in the temple and threw out all the market traders, his enemies decided that now was the time to get him arrested. They wanted to kill him. But it wasn't easy. The ordinary people loved Jesus. His enemies were afraid that if they arrested him the people would riot.

So day by day, with Jesus teaching at the temple, and crowds listening, they tried to trap him. They kept trying to get him to say something wrong, to get him into trouble. They failed. Jesus answered all their questions.

But then Jesus' enemies got the chance they were looking for. For some reason Judas, one of Jesus' twelve disciples, decided to help them arrest him. They agreed to pay Judas thirty silver coins if he would lead them to a place, away from the crowds, where they could arrest Jesus.

NOW LOOK AT:

What happened when Jesus was arrested? p81
Did Jesus get bullied? p83
Why did Jesus get angry in the temple? p33
Who were Jesus' enemies? p72

What did Jesus do on the night before he died?

I wonder what you would do if you knew you only had one more day to live? Whatever you chose to do, it would show what you thought was important in your life.

What Jesus did was to gather all his friends together. Then they had one last meal. At the meal Jesus took a piece of bread. "Imagine this is me," he said. And as they watched, he broke the bread. It was his way of showing that he was going to die the next day.

Then he took some wine. "Imagine this is my blood," he said. And as they watched, he poured it out. It was his way of showing how he would bleed when they nailed him to the cross.

He told his friends to have this simple meal as a way of remembering him. So today, across the world, Christians still break bread and drink wine together. It's their way of remembering Jesus, and the last meal he had before he died.

NOW LOOK AT:

Who were Jesus' friends? p25
Did Jesus know he was going to die? p77
Could Jesus pray anywhere? p64
Was Jesus ever afraid? p74

What happened when Jesus was arrested?

On the evening that he was arrested, Jesus had one last meal with his friends. While they were eating, Jesus told them that one of them would help his enemies to find him. He told them that when he was arrested, they would all run away.

His friend Peter was angry. He told Jesus he was ready to die with him. Jesus told Peter that before the cock crowed, he would say three times that he didn't know Jesus.

After their meal they went to a garden called Gethsemane. It was the dead of night. Jesus was praying for strength when a large crowd sent by the chief priests arrived, with swords and clubs.

Judas, one of Jesus' friends, came up and kissed Jesus. This was a secret signal, to show the crowd which one to arrest. They seized Jesus, and all his friends ran away.

Peter followed at a distance. But when people asked if he was Jesus' friend he became afraid. He said three times that he didn't know him. Then the cock crowed. Peter remembered what Jesus had said at the meal. He broke down and wept.

NOW LOOK AT:

Why did Jesus come into our world? p40

When did Jesus pray? p59

Was Jesus ever afraid? p74

see Mark chapter 15, verses 6–15

Who said Jesus had to die?

After Jesus was arrested, he was taken to the house of the High Priest, Caiaphas (*Kye-a-fass*). There, a special meeting was called to see if Jesus ought to die.

The thing was, they couldn't find any real reason to kill him. People came in and told lies about Jesus, but even their lies didn't agree with each other.

Finally the High Priest asked Jesus straight out: "Are you the Messiah – the Son of God?" "I am," said Jesus. And the High Priest was furious. He tore his robes, showing that he thought Jesus should die.

But only the Romans could put someone to death. So the priests dragged Jesus off to Pilate, the Roman governor. Pilate spoke to Jesus and decided he had done nothing wrong.

He wanted to set Jesus free. But instead the crowd demanded that Pilate set free a man called Barabbas – a murderer. They demanded that Jesus should be nailed to the cross.

Pilate was afraid a riot might start. So he set the murderer free and told his soldiers to kill Jesus.

NOW LOOK AT:

How did Jesus die? p84

What is a Christian? p89

What does the name 'Jesus' mean? p13

Did Jesus do anything wrong? p75

Did Jesus get bullied?

Eventually Jesus' enemies had him taken prisoner and put him on trial. They wanted to get rid of him, to kill him. After Jesus' first trial, he was bullied by a group of people. They blindfolded him, then took it in turns to hit him. "If you're so special," they said, "tell us which one of us hit you that time!"

Then, after Pilate said that Jesus had to die, a group of soldiers decided to have some fun with him. They called all the soldiers together so they could all have a laugh.

They pretended that Jesus was their king. They dressed him in purple – the king's colour. They made a painful crown out of thorns and pushed it onto his head. They made him hold a reed, as if it were a king's sceptre. They pretended to bow down to him, and mocked him. Then they spat on him, and hit him round the head.

All this time Jesus said nothing. The only time he said anything about the soldiers was to ask God to forgive them when they nailed him to the cross.

NOW LOOK AT:

What's so special about Jesus? p8
Why did Jesus have to die? p85
Was Jesus ever sad? p69
What did Jesus teach about forgiveness? p53

see Matthew chapter 27, verses 45–54

How did Jesus die?

The part of the Roman Empire where Jesus lived was ruled by Roman soldiers. The Romans had a terrible way of killing people who had done wrong. They nailed them to wooden crosses by their hands and feet and left them to die. This was called crucifixion.

Although he had done nothing wrong, Jesus was sentenced to death. After his trial, Roman soldiers flogged him and forced him to carry a heavy length of wood to the top of a hill.

There, they nailed Jesus to the piece of wood, and hoisted him up to a stake, high above the ground, to make a cross. Jesus was crucified with two thieves, one on each side of him.

His friends looked on helplessly as Jesus hung there. At midday, the sky went black for three hours. His last words were: "It is finished". Then a Roman soldier made sure he was dead by stabbing his side with a sword.

One of Jesus' friends, Joseph of Arimathea, asked if he could have the dead body for burial. He buried Jesus' body in a cave cut out of rock, and rolled a heavy stone over the entrance.

NOW LOOK AT:

What happened at the first Easter? p86
Who were Jesus' friends? p25
What happened when someone died? p44
Did Jesus do anything wrong? p75

see Romans chapter 5, verse 8

Why did Jesus have to die?

All of us do things that are wrong. It might be stealing something. It might be telling lies. It might be being cruel to someone.

Those wrong things give God a problem. He wants to forgive us. But he can't just say, "There, there – it doesn't matter." It does matter when we are cruel to each other.

That's where Jesus steps in. He knows that the only way people can get close to God is to have their "sin" (all the bad things they have done) taken away. And he offered to take the punishment for them.

It wasn't easy. In fact, Jesus spent the whole night before he died, praying. He knew it would be terrible to be nailed to a cross.

But in some mysterious way the death of Jesus was part of God's plan. When Jesus died on the cross, it meant that each person who wants to can be forgiven, and start a new life, knowing that God is their Father.

NOW LOOK AT:

What's so special about Jesus?	*p8*
How does God feel about us?	*p50*
Was Jesus ever afraid?	*p74*

What happened at the first Easter?

After Jesus' death, he was buried in a cave. A huge piece of rock was rolled across the entrance.

Two days later, three women who were Jesus' friends went to put spices on his body. They were worried about how to move the heavy rock.

But when they got there, it had already been moved! An angel told them that God had made Jesus come alive again and told them to go and tell Jesus' friends.

When his friends, Peter and John, ran to Jesus' grave they found the grave clothes they had wrapped him in, but his body had gone.

Later, they found out why. They met Jesus again: in a garden; on a road; by a lake. They didn't meet a dead man and they didn't meet a ghost. Jesus had been dead, but now he was alive again. God had raised him from death.

When we give each other Easter eggs, it reminds us of what happened at the first Easter. An egg looks dead. But if a chicken sits on it and warms it, new life bursts out. It reminds us that Jesus came alive out of his grave.

NOW LOOK AT:

Can dead people really come back to life?	*p90*
How do we know Jesus isn't just a story?	*p16*
Is Jesus God's son?	*p15*
How do we know that Jesus rose from the dead?	*p91*

see John chapter 14, verses 25,26

Does Jesus still live on earth?

On the night before Jesus died, he gathered his friends together for one final meal. There he explained that he would soon be leaving them and going to heaven to be with God his Father.

His friends were sad and confused. They didn't want Jesus to leave them. But he promised to send them another helper – his Holy Spirit – who would be with them always.

When Jesus died, his friends were heartbroken. When they met him again and found that he was alive, they were overjoyed. But several weeks later came the moment Jesus had told them about at their last supper. Jesus was taken from them into heaven. His final words were that they should do nothing but wait until God had given them the Holy Spirit.

So Jesus is still alive... but not on this earth. Today he is in heaven, with God his Father, but his Holy Spirit is with everyone who is a follower of Jesus.

NOW LOOK AT:

Can dead people really come back to life? p90

What did Jesus teach about heaven? p65

How do we know that Jesus rose from the dead? p91

What did Jesus do on the night before he died? p80

Who is the Holy Spirit?

Just before Jesus left his friends to go to heaven, he told them to wait in Jerusalem for God to send them his "helper" – the Holy Spirit.

The disciples did as Jesus told them. They went to Jerusalem and waited... for about ten days. Then, on a special Harvest Festival day called Pentecost, the disciples were all together. Suddenly they heard a powerful wind blowing. And they saw what looked like flames. These were signs from God: he was sending them his Holy Spirit, who was going to help them.

The Holy Spirit brings the power of God to the life of a follower of Jesus.

The Holy Spirit certainly helped Jesus' friends. Before, they had been in hiding, frightened of what would happen to them. Now that the Holy Spirit was helping them, they bravely went out onto the streets and told everyone that Jesus was alive. Thousands of people believed them and became Christians: followers of Jesus Christ.

NOW LOOK AT:

How do I find out more about Jesus?	*p92*
Who is Jesus?	*p7*
How do we know that Jesus isn't just a story?	*p16*

What is a Christian?

At the start of the three years Jesus spent telling people about God, he was walking along the edge of the lake. He met two fishermen called Simon and Andrew. He challenged them and said, "Follow me," and they did. They left everything and spent the rest of their lives as Jesus' followers.

Today, following Jesus means to try to live like him, to listen to what he says, and to try to do it. Jesus promised to give his Holy Spirit to his followers, to change them and to help them live good lives.

Someone who follows Jesus is called a Christian. It doesn't mean that they are perfect. It does mean that they are trying to live like Jesus.

Christians believe that because of Jesus' death they have been forgiven for all the wrong they have done.

Christians read about God and Jesus in the Bible, and try to live as the Bible teaches them.

Christians pray to God about things other people need. They give money to God and work to make the world a better place for poor, hungry and ill people.

These are just some of the things it means to follow Jesus.

NOW LOOK AT:

Who were Jesus' friends? p25

Who is the Holy Spirit? p88

What did Jesus say about human beings? p66

Can dead people really come back to life?

Think how amazing your body is. It takes strength from food; when you cut yourself, cells repair the damage; when you put your hand in scalding water you jerk it out again without thinking.

The human body is such a wonderful thing, it could never have made itself. It was designed by God, who gave you the gift of life.

But think about it: if your life is God's gift, how could death end it?

In fact, it doesn't. Jesus taught that although your body dies, the real "you" lives on, only in another form.

Jesus' friends knew that. They met Jesus after he had died. He proved he wasn't a ghost by actually eating with them. He promised them that after they died, they would have a new "perfect" body, and will live with him, in heaven.

Can dead people really come back to life? Of course! Life is the gift of our powerful God. And if God put our life there... who can take it away?!

NOW LOOK AT:

What did Jesus teach about heaven?	*p65*
Why did Jesus make sick people well?	*p71*
Does Jesus still live on earth?	*p87*

How do we know that Jesus rose from the dead?

Not everyone believes that Jesus rose from the dead. Some people say his friends stole his body and then made the whole thing up. But that can't be true! Some of Jesus' friends were killed for saying that Jesus was alive. People don't die for a lie.

Other people think that Jesus' enemies stole the body. But the last thing his enemies wanted was for people to think that Jesus was alive again!

So how do we know that Jesus rose from the dead? We just need to look at what happened to his friends.

When Jesus was arrested, his friends were very frightened. They ran away into hiding. But weeks later, there they were in the Jerusalem city centre, telling everyone that Jesus was alive, and that they had met him.

What happened to change them from frightened, hiding people into a group prepared to risk death by saying that Jesus was alive? Christians believe that what happened is what all the eye-witnesses tell us happened: Jesus was raised from the dead and is alive today!

NOW LOOK AT:

How do we know that Jesus isn't just a story? p16

What happened at the first Easter? p86

Does Jesus still live on earth? p87

How do I find out more about Jesus?

First, you could buy your own Bible. Look for one in a modern version, that you can understand. The Good News Bible is one of the best translations for children. Towards the front of your Bible you'll find a contents page. Look for "Matthew", "Mark", "Luke" and "John". These are the four Gospels – they tell the story of what Jesus said and did. Start by reading Mark, the simplest and shortest of the Gospels.

Second, if you don't already belong to a church, find one near you and join it. Look for one where there's lots going on for young people of your age.

Third, at your school there may be a group for Christians. If there is someone in your class or tutor group who is a Christian ask them to tell you where they go to church, and whether there is a group for Christians at your school. If there is, why not join it? If there isn't, why not ask if one of the teachers will start one?

NOW LOOK AT:

What did Jesus teach about heaven? p65

Did Jesus go to church? p19

How does God feel about us? p50

Index

Another **Snapshots** *book for you to enjoy!*

Puzzle Teaser

Can you crack the codes, solve the wordsearches and find your way through the mazes?

Pick up a pen and start puzzling your way through the Bible!

ISBN 1 85999 286 2
£2.99

Available from your local Christian Bookshop